Illustrations: Erin McChesney

ISBN   978-1-951448-04-2   E-book $9.99
ISBN   978-1-951448-03-5   Paperback $14.99

Please enjoy The White Devil & the Twisted, Young Owl,
—Megan

The White Devil & The Twisted, Young Owl

Megan Schreiber-Carter

I

The Way We Were

II

Fending Off

III

The Way It Is

Chapter 1
The Way We Were

I
Kicked Out of Complacency

The White Devil wound down his whirlwind, where the woods ended and my porch began. In one, final bound, he stepped out of his whirl, his foot hit the floor, and he was on the porch with us. Big chest heaving from obvious exertion, his brow flushed and furrowed, he shifted into the shade, escaping the summer-afternoon sun. He sure was winded. Pressing his backside against the house, he braced his hunched torso with his hands on his thighs.

"**You two gotta** *come* **with** *me*," the Devil managed to insist to the floor, where he'd fixed his stare. Over-taxed as he was, he'd still kept a hold of his single-minded approach to attaining his current goal.

A hulking, Latvian-American by birth, an instinctual outdoorsman, a mighty hunter, and a Harley rider, the Devil also had grown-up tuned-in to the 1970s, D.C.-ghetto culture. All this showed as his keen, blue eyes rose and scanned the area. His eyes landed and locked on the place where I sat with our old friend Sterling.

Always-gentle Sterling and I looked up at him from our near beers, served in honor of Sterling's struggle to stay off the sauce. We'd just had a toast to Sterling's success at avoiding what Sterling called his "next, romantic relationshit." Unfortunately, Sterling hadn't found luck in love, in his life. Both bare-footed and "airin' our dogs," he and I'd been peaceful here without the Devil. But, now, here he was, irked, and poking us.

The Devil was into something, was ON to *something*. He desperately wanted to be talking—you could see it in his fierce glare. But, instead, he dipped his head and slid into a bit of a squat, still trying to recover his breath.

Slowly, Sterling turned his weathered face, well-wrinkled from sun and booze, towards me. Sterling raised an eyebrow. He eased off the cap of his next near beer and enjoyed a swig. Otherwise, we didn't budge. We were used to the Devil's impulsive calls to action. The only thing new here was his lack of breath.

So, I wasn't worried about the Devil and neither was Sterling, who was often a good gauge of emergency situations. Not only was Sterling a battle-weary, grounded, medevac-helicopter pilot, he was also the son of a reverend minister. He and I'd been sitting, discussing life—his always draped in melodious Tennessee-isms. We'd been deep into our ongoing efforts to exorcise our own demons, aiming to find some meaning or hope that helps make some sense of things—until now. Until the appearance of the White Devil—who we also call our "old-friend Erik," and who I also call "my brother-in-law."

Erik's sudden appearance is rarely unexpected. We all know he tends to show up instantly. These days, a sighting was even more likely, since, lately, Erik had taken to running off some of his excess energy along the deer trails through my neighborhood.

"There's this **owl**," Erik spat in a rush of breath. "Ya *gotta* **see** *him!*" Then, there he was—breathless again. Sterling grinned tolerantly, gently nodded his great head of dark-brown-and-graying hair. I grinned with him.

Sterling was gracious company. He had a way of being decent. It's nice just to be around that. He even smelled great. He wore the best deep, clean cologne. Many times, giving him a hug, I'd told him, "you *smell* **great**." I'd seen other women say it to him, too. He always smiled pleasantly and usually moved on to his charming habit of looking attentively into your eyes when he spoke with you. This was the same charming way his late father had had, when speaking with others. And, Sterling, named after his father, as the fourth of this name in his family's line, actually enjoyed sitting and having good, earnest conversation. What's not to like?

Erik tried for a deep breath but got only a bit.

"Water, Erik?" I asked, pulling a bottle from my bag. He nodded, reached over, grabbed it, got in a sip, got another bit of breath, got in another sip. Then, he dipped his head again.

We call Erik the "White Devil" not because he's a *bad* guy, not *really*, but because an elderly lady semi-affectionately dubbed him with the title. It fit, all too well, not only his very-white appearance but also his sometimes-questionable morality and his devilish tendency to laugh, without regard, at human failings others do **NOT** find funny. He's even been known to tempt others' vices—taking pastries to fat people, cigarettes to smokers, insults to the irritable, hard liquor to heavy drinkers…. Some quirk in Erik compelled him to find sport in the weaknesses of others.

Erik looked up.

"You two don't **get it,**" he burst out with frustration. "*It's* **weird.**"

"Whaat's weird?" Sterling asked evenly in his caressing, Tennessee tones before taking another clean sip, despite today's relatively mild tremors in his hands.

"**The owl!**" Erik boomed. He stood up. He huffed-out used-up air, was obviously irritated by our passivity. I settled more comfortably into my chair, to conserve energy, to prepare for the campaign Erik would now wage. I pointed Erik's attention to a folded chair he might want.

Ignoring me, Erik still stood, still wild eyed, still catching his breath. He was a handsome devil. They both were—God help the two of them and all the women of the earth. More than just easy on the eyes, they were also the world-wise children of attractive, bright parents who'd found success in the capital city of the U.S., just a few miles down the road. To meet the two of them, though, you'd never know they'd grown up together in D.C. because they both tended to country ways, somehow left over from their grandparents. We three shared country ways, but I was the only one of us who'd actually grown up in the country.

Erik took in three, deep breaths. The last one came out evenly. He now had a hold of himself. "*Listen!*" Erik insisted. "I was joggin' on the trail, along the ridge by Cabin John Creek, when right in front of me runs this **fox.** *Middle a the afternoon!* So, I look around and I see these two **owls** flappin', **screamin'**, scarin' it off, ya know? Sterling nodded politely as we listened to Erik's rapid, spirited tale. Erik almost whispered this next bit, "*Then, there he is, on the ground*—**this young owl.** Big! Like, *not* a baby but *not* an adult, ya know? And there's **somethin' weird** *about him!*" Deadly serious and clearly stumped, Erik stared at us in silence.

"I don't know," I said, "some kind of owl distemper or rabies, maybe. Fear alone—"

"**No!**" Erik yelled loud enough to be heard for a quarter mile. "The owl's **twisted** somehow! He was *kinda* looking at me, but his head's all cocked. *It's up-side down!* It's **NOT** *NORMAL!*"

Sterling and I exchanged glances. It'd been a long time since the White Devil had imbibed anything stronger than a near beer himself, but, you know, flashbacks, and stuff like that, can happen.

"He *may* get **better**," Sterling drawled softly, as he often did about Erik, "but he'll **never** get *well*." I smiled as we returned our eyes to the still-irritated, nearly-frothing White Devil. "Ya *gotta* calm *down*, Erik," Sterling advised soothingly.

"*Shove* it, Sterling," the Devil countered but with less volume.

"Can't hurt me, Erik," Sterling replied, casually. "I'm all *scaarr* tissue." I smiled again. Erik frowned some more.

"That fox was *preyin'* on that baby owl!" Erik let out with now-sober urgency. "Was three *steps* from *eatin'* him, '*till he saw* **me**! The vultures are *comin'*! We gotta go get him!*"

"Call animal control," Sterling continued, as a soft voice of reason. "They're experts—"

"No, man! I'm *tellin'* ya—**he's not gonna last!**"

"Erik," I indulged him, "*even* if we *went*, how the *hell* would we get it outta there? Can't just pick it up and walk—"

"Yeah, thought about that. Bet they're *painful peckers*. And, *hell*, if the baby didn't *claw* me to death, the *parents would! They're swoopin'*," he emphasized with an amused relative of a laugh in his voice.

"Great," I replied, first nodding and then shaking my head.

"We *gotta* **try**," urged Erik, the tempter. There was something in his voice, some kind of plea. For all his wild burliness, the White Devil seemed like a lost kid begging for help. I knew him to have such callous irreverence for *human* weaknesses that his drive to help this young owl was refreshing, heartwarming.

"Well," Sterling offered kindly, as he seemed to feel it, too, "we *could* throw a *blanket* over it."

"*Right!*" Erik replied. "And, we need a box."

"My neighbor's cat carrier," I volunteered, while pulling on my socks, because now, somehow, I was in it, too.

"Yep," Erik said, nodding with approval at his recruits and heading off the porch, while Sterling worked his feet into his own socks.

"Hang *on*," I told the Devil, as I stepped into rubber boots. "We need gloves, a blanket, a broom—"

"What's the broom for?" Sterling asked. Swiftly, he drained his bottle as he, too, stood. I looked up the half-a-dozen inches to his uncertain, deep-brown eyes.

"To keep the *parents* off *us*," I warned him. Sterling ran his fingers through his thick hair, the way he does when he's flustered. He grinned sadly. Then, Sterling pulled in a deep breath, letting it out evenly as he gave me a series of accepting, supportive nods.

2
And, Away We Go...

The White Devil didn't know the neighborhood's streets as well as I did, but he described the terrain, near the owls, so well that I suspected I'd parked us pretty close to the spot. As soon as we hiked through a bit of woods, I knew we'd meet right up with the forested, deer trail and the rushing creek just beyond it.

Having already opened my car's hatch, Erik grabbed the rolled-up blanket. Much like a deer, he bounded into the nearby brush and on into deeper woods.

Sterling, with the cat carrier full of gloves, and I, with the broom, headed in at a crisp pace that clearly wasn't crisp enough for the Devil. Erik stopped up ahead, just long enough to glare back at us and groan in frustration. Tucking the cream-colored blanket farther up, under his arm, the Devil shot off once more, leaping over felled tree trunks and brush like the wild thing he is. What stood out most were his muscular calves, bounding with agility beneath the long, white, strings, dangling from his jean shorts, ripped-off just above his knees.

Erik reached the deer trail, looked to the tree tops, and darted south. By the time we were half-way to the trail, he'd returned to his starting point and was now quickly headed north, yelling *"this way!"*

"Ohhh," Sterling groaned. Sterling stopped and looked down at the tangle of brush raking raw the sides of his high-end, street boots. He pulled loose, cursed "...*damn vines an' poison ivy...*" under his breath, and stepped much more carefully.

Erik stopped long enough to yell through the woods, *"come on, **Sterling**, ya lazy bastard. Stop **swishin'** through the woods and get **over** here! **Why** did we **even BRING** you!?"*

Sterling's irritation was clear in his frown. "Let's kill the Viking," Sterling grumbled as he picked up his pace. I burst out laughing. "If I *clock him* with this *carrier*," he said, holding it up, "will ya *help* me bury the *body*?" I laughed out loud, again, but nodded sympathetically, attempting to soften the White Devil's rude comments. I wasn't much faster; I didn't know why I'd been spared the abuse.

Once on the trail, Sterling managed to flash me a newly firm-and-determined grin. I was *pretty* sure we weren't headed in to attack the White Devil, but the thought of it made me laugh again.

"*Here!*" Erik urged, in a brief, harsh hush, and repeatedly, until we arrived next to him. With him, we fixed our attention where he pointed, at the base of a leaf-buried tree. The tree was about twenty feet before us and on a gentle, upward slope. I saw nothing, not until we all looked up the length of the *very* tall tree.

There I saw one, well-clawed parent, flying, silently, with four feet of wings. It had dipped deeply down but was now headed back to the top. The other parent was in a nest there, calling loudly, "*ick, ick, ick, ick....,*" in an agitated, rasping hiss.

"*Damn,*" I breathed out, "those are some *big* birds."

As we watched, the nested owl's complaints picked up in pace and volume, "*ICK, ICK, ICK, ICK....*" Then, I heard a heart-stopping, cat-like screech from the flyer, as it landed near its partner.

My eyes on the parents, I felt Erik slap a pair of gloves against my arm and heard a pair hit Sterling's chest. The parents continued with their sounds of alarm but more like squeaky toys worn out from too much use. We pulled on our gloves, as the owls now hooted— sounding like "Who cooks for you? Who cooks for you?" I heard no more screeching. But, of course, they didn't have to bark much—not with the kinds of claws *they* had and an address sixty feet in the air.

"*There,*" Erik insisted with that same urgent hush that demanded we look. Leaving Erik on attack-watch, I risked a peek at the ground where he pointed. "*See him!?!*"

I didn't, probably because I was unwilling to take my eyes completely off the parents, but if Erik said it was there, I was sure it was. Erik had hunter's eyes, could see things others overlooked.

Then, a blink revealed two, big, beautiful, wide-opened eyes. There it was, standing stock-still even as its form unblended from the dried leaves around it. It looked to be about a fourth the size of the adults. I frowned as I processed a convoluted image—its neck bent off to its right side in an arc, its head oriented upside down and facing me, though I was looking at its back. It saw the world backwards, upside down, and from about half-way down the right side of its body. The head seemed *fixed* that way. Just *looking* at it was painful.

"*Thaaat owl's fuuckked up,*" Sterling whispered slowly as we all stood frozen.

"Is it," I whispered back, "is its neck—*broken?*"

"*Don't know,*" Erik whispered urgently.

"Is there *blood?*" Sterling asked. "Maybe it's in *pain.*"

"Don't see *blood,*" Erik snapped, "and he's *not* cryin'."

"And, what's it sound like when *owls* cry?" Sterling asked but got no answer. "Injured creatures can be *noble,*" Sterling whispered. "They often *hide* their pain."

"Moving it could *kill* it," I said. Erik offered a frustrated huff of breath but kept his attention on the tree tops.

"If we *don't* move him," Erik argued quickly, without once looking at us, "we kill him for *sure.* Least he won't die gettin' torn apart by *whatever's comin' next to eat him!*" The White Devil still had that point, and he'd latched onto it like a pit bull on a bone. I looked to Sterling, who shrugged.

"*Tough call,*" Sterling said. "Maybe there's some *special* way. Maybe, if we call a *vet.*" He felt for his phone but didn't find it and resorted to running his gloved hand through his messed-up hair.

"*Screw **that**!*" Erik erupted in that harsh whisper. He glanced from the parents and snapped, "**We** *get **him** outta **here*** before the **parents GET US!**"

But, there was silence and stillness from above.

"***Wait***," I insisted. "A fall like that should've killed it. Maybe it *can* fly, a *little.*" I urged them both back, under the cover of a low, pine bough. Erik frowned and shook his head at this threatened mutiny. "It's lived this long," I argued. "Maybe it's *learning* to fly. Maybe it can *claw* its way up the tree."

"If he could do *that,* he'd be *up* there," Erik insisted, as if it were common sense, and he was probably right. Erik looked back up with disgust, seemed convinced the entire world was full of idiots. Sterling focused on the grounded owl, as it looked back at us with wide eyes. I considered it with him.

"*Well,*" Sterling offered thoughtfully, "even if *their* necks **can** do that, I doubt his *wings* can do more than *break* his descent. Don't see how he *can* fly, not with his *head* like that—reversed reference points, mechanics compromised, equilibrium off. *No,* **look** at him. Somethin's *really* wrong. If he just had his *first* flight, it's his *last.* Don't think he **can** fly *or* crawl up that tree. *Doubt* he ever *could,*" he added sadly.

"**So**," Erik announced without looking from the parents, "we **get** him." Erik unrolled the blanket.

"He's *grounded*," Sterling concluded with empathy, "**stranded**, *only alive* by the *grace* a God an' the *care* of his parents."

"But," I insisted, with a restraining hand on Erik's forearm, "*somehow*, he lives here. He's wild. Maybe it's best to let wild things **be** *wild*."

"Not if it's **killin'** him!" Erik argued before flashing me his dominating stare.

"How's it *killing* him? I persisted. "If the parents are *feeding* him, if they're *protecting* him—"

"Not too **well** an' for **how long**?" Erik demanded. I considered that. I wondered how long he'd been on the ground. Night was coming. All this did have the feel of life or death for him. Eventually, something's going to do each of us in, but, if I could prevent it, I was unwilling to let *this* be the young owl's fate.

"*Any* chance at life is better than *this* death?" I asked Sterling. He smiled slightly and nodded just enough that I found myself joining him. "What's the plan then?" I asked.

"**Get the damn owl,**" Erik pronounced curtly as Sterling sighed, nodded some more, and opened wide the carrier's door.

"*Smart*, Sterling," I said encouragingly and surprisingly evenly, considering my now-rapid heart beat. "Erik, **you** throw the blanket, scoop him up—*gently*—and slide him in. **I'll** keep the parents off with the broom."

"*Now*, **Erik**," Sterling warned him, with a gloved finger pointing right in the Devil's face, "no ready, fire, aim. *Eaaassy* does it."

"**Go!**" Erik commanded and took off.

"**Oock, Oock,**" it was a high-pitched, lonesome, desperate, echoing, rasping squawk, suddenly coming from *both* parents. Sterling and I took simultaneous, deep breaths. We followed our determined, fearless leader, who had their baby scooped and in the carrier before Sterling and I had completely reached him. I looked up.

With a screeching cry, I felt in my bones, the parents dove. I saw them aim their talons at us. My heart raced. Using a firm grip, I swatted furiously at the air between us and the closest of the ferocious owls, whose great wings, somehow, flapped *noiselessly* above us.

I *made* myself believe I *could* win, and maybe that's why I did. I discouraged them from their targets, causing both to swoop back up again before I saw Erik slam the door, throw the blanket at Sterling, and take off with the carrier.

"Ho-ly *shhiit*," Sterling breathed out, with his chin in the air. I looked up and saw the huge parents begin another dive. They were staggering the attack this time. One was yards ahead of the other, who'd just paused on a branch. Sterling and I backed away from the spot, with Sterling draping the abandoned blanket above our heads. God bless him, Sterling stuck with me. Though it was tough to see above the blanket, I swung the broom violently. I didn't *want* to hit them or hurt them. I *hated* what we were doing to them, didn't *blame* them, just wanted to discourage *them* from hurting *us*.

Chapter II

Fending Off

I
Fending for Ourselves

Desperately, I swatted less than a foot from the talons of the owl engaged in the closest dive. I heard Sterling's heavy breath next to my ear, as I tripped, as I felt him grab my shoulder, as we both fell backwards only a few inches from claws as long as my fingers. Attack postponed, both parents headed back to the top of the trees. I stood with Sterling's grip pulling me up by my armpit and all four of our eyes on the parents.

"*I'll watch our way* **out**," he announced. "**You** watch **them**." It was the kind of crisp, sensible command you hear and follow in an emergency.

"*Right*," I breathed, while he pulled me along by my shirt collar, while each came at us *again in a staggered attack*, while, *again*, I swatted.

"*It's the blanket!*" Sterling announced, as he threw it away. After that, he pushed me ahead of him and we ran after the White Devil.

I tried to keep us under the pine boughs. The parents followed, from a distance high in the trees. They continued to accuse and convict us, but didn't swoop again.

My hand pulled on the car's door handle. My lungs burned from exertion. The White Devil lounged comfortably in the front-passenger's seat, laughing loudly, as he watched us jump inside. Behind the safety of the car's closed windows, I scanned the heavens.

"Did they **get** *ya?*" Erik asked, highly amused and letting out a long-and-loud, devil-may-care laugh at our frantic plight. I suddenly suspected the Devil knew, full well, that the cream blanket was likely a target that could distract the parents from *him* to focus in on *us*.

"**No**," I snapped, causing him to laugh even harder. As I still stared aloft, I located the perched parents. "It's exhausting," I announced over the heart pounding in my chest.

"They, they **are** *flyin' sloppy*," Sterling offered from the back, through deep drags of breath. "They're, they're *battle weary* all right," he concluded as we all watched them watch us.

Then, I smelled it. "*Ewww-h*, what the *hell* is *that?*" I asked and covered my nose.

"*Oh yeah,*" said the Devil with more of his wild-and-hearty laugh. "*He sure does stink. Car's* gonna **reek** of it," he added. He laughed some more as Sterling and I looked back to the carrier, secured in the hatch.

2
Mesmerizer

We settled the twisted, young owl, still in the carrier, on a table, in the corner of my porch, and covered all but the front of the cage with a blanket. Hanging up his phone call to a wildlife-rescue league, Erik announced, "I'm takin' him out there first thing in the morning."

"What can we **do** for him?" Sterling asked kindly.

"Keep things calm," Erik replied with the satisfied tone of a warrior in the welcome ease that follows successful battle. "Make some oatmeal, maybe make a paste with insects. Put it on a plate. Prob'ly won't eat it, though. Prob'ly can't."

With a sad look on her face, my ten-year-old daughter watched the owl carefully. She whispered, "what happened to him?"

"We—don't know," I admitted.

"Why does he stink like that?" she whispered, as she and I peered into the carrier, where the silent, little guy stood, tucked into the back corner, with his front toward us and his face tight to the corner.

"Throws up on himself, I bet," her Uncle Erik replied. "Food just rots on him, I think." Then, Erik, too, bent and peered in, before her "Nearly-Uncle Sterling" joined us. "Called a Barred Owl," Erik added in a firm whisper.

"Bard?" I asked. "Like a poet?"

"**Barrrred**," Erik emphasized, as if I were an idiot, "'cause a those **bars** on him." With that, the attractive white lines and baby fuzz highlighting his grey feathers mesmerized us all....

3
Eye Candy

Word about the twisted, young owl spread to the neighborhood kids like an offer of free candy. Soon, we had a steady parade of curiosity-seeking little people surrounding the porch.

"One at a time and quietly," I whispered before they peered in, in turn. The twisted owl didn't appear to want to go anywhere, so I left the cage door open and the blanket draped around the opening. This way, the kids didn't need to get so close to see him well. The first kids were younger. They kept a wary, silent distance from the young animal, who was still tucked in and facing that far corner and still, still as a statue. I figured that stillness had helped him survive, so I told the kids that.

"Would he like some tea?" whispered the littlest girl in the group.

"Thanks for the thought, honey," I told her, "but I don't think he drinks tea." She nodded sadly and backed away from her turn at seeing him. "You could catch a bug for him, though," I suggested. She nodded happily and headed off to do that.

"*Ick*," "*eeee*," "*yuck*," "*ewww....*" These sounds shot out of the older, bolder kids' mouths as they gawked in at him, in turn. Mostly, the owl faced away, into that corner. Once or twice, though, in a sudden, noisy fluster of feathers, the sad, big-eyed creature awkwardly turned his trunk a bit. Whenever this happened, the current viewer gasped.

Concerned it would freak the little guy out even more, I didn't allow any pictures—I was sometimes sorry about that later. At the time, though, I shared what I figured were the mixed-up feelings of a zookeeper—I was willing to let them see him but I needed to protect them from from each other.

"He doesn't hoot," one kid announced. He was right. Through it all, the young owl never uttered a sound. But, there was no peace in the quiet, only tension. When he faced into that corner for long periods, I worried—*is* he still alive?

"His head's flopped over," one peering kid criticized, with a frown.

"He's lookin' at me *upside down!*" another said with wonder. We were smart enough to occupy all non-viewing kids with finding, grinding and mixing insects into spring water and cooked oatmeal. Soon, we had more bug mush than we'd *ever* need, but we encouraged them to keep at it, keep off the porch, and keep away from the owl. And, honestly, I lied to the kids. I told them the owl was leaving at nightfall. I didn't want them coming back when he was out here alone.

"It's *ugly*. It *stinks*. We should *kill* it," one burly boy insisted as he suddenly began poking inside the cage with a stick.

"**No**," Sterling barked, jumped up and grabbed the stick from the kid. "You don't *kill* something just 'cause it's *wounded*."

"*It can't even fly,*" the kid barked back.

"*That doesn't* **matter**," Sterling insisted. "*He's still* **alive**."

"For *what?* It's *stupid!*"

"*Is* **that** *right!?*" Sterling demanded, red faced with anger I'd *never* seen in him. "The owl's **stupid?**"

"It's **STUPID**," the boy insisted.

"**Yer** *stupid*," Sterling spat at him.

"**Yer stupid!**" the kid shot back.

"Give it up, Sterling," Erik said, laughing. "Ya can't fix *stupid*."

The boy gave both men a dirty look before heading off the porch, in a huff, to join the intent crew of insect murderers in the yard.

4
In the Silent Night

I couldn't rest. Somewhere around 3 a.m., I pulled on a sweatshirt and headed out to the porch, in the silent night. Quietly, I opened the cage and slipped the blanket back just enough to see the owl's back. From there, my eyes followed the impossible curve of his neck, bent over in an upside-down-U shape and ending with his surreal, upside-down head, off to his side. Above his closed eyes, his firm beak helped reorient me to his inverted features. He was motionless, completely still in that back corner, but his twisted body was dotted with the oatmeal-bug mush, which maybe, somehow, he'd been able to eat. That thought allowed me to *hope* he was only asleep.

His amber eyes slid open, causing me to catch my breath and freeze. He had to be scared but seemed calm. For him, I figured, this *was* calm—poor little, baby thing. I wondered how many times, just in the last day, he'd faced his death with his magnificent, twisted head, backwards, upside-down, and off to his side. I breathed easier, tried to be glad that *maybe* we'd made his life better, *maybe* we'd brought some hope to this hopeless creature.

As I watched him, his wide, glowing eyes gathered and returned to me the bit of light shining in to him from the moon. Those beautiful, big, soulful eyes—searching, searching for answers, as we all are all of our lives. He looked so intelligent, innocent, stoic, fragile, and dignified all at the same time. When his eyes bravely locked with mine, I wondered—is he *actually insightful? Could* he *be* wise enough to reason through *any* of this?

This crippled, silent creature couldn't seem to make *any* sounds. He couldn't even utter a simple "who," let alone any of the other questions arising from his existence—"*Where* am I? *Why* am I trapped? *How* do I get free? *Who* will help me?" And, who could tell who? Ultimately, our lives are so oddly intertwined with what life presents us.

Chapter III

The Way It Is

I
Tree Rats

The White Devil took our silent owl away, first thing the next morning, and I missed the little creature's presence immediately. The Devil called, on his way back from the wildlife rescue, to report.

"...said he *wasn't* injured," Erik told me, "said he was *born* this way."

"A birth defect?"

"Yep. They've seen others like this. Sometimes the moms push 'em out, when they know they're defective. Sometimes they just grow 'till they fall out a the nest, 'cause they're too big but they can't fly."

"It's common?"

"They're seein' more of it."

"Is he in pain?"

"Ahhh, don't *think* so."

"Don't know how he *couldn't* be."

"Ah, yeah, probably," Erik admitted. "*They've got painkillers.*"

"Erik, will he *live?*"

"They'll do what they can."

"That's *all* you got from them?"

"That's *all* they had to **tell** me," he barked dismissively. "I was in a *hurry*. They're gonna *call* me," he concluded. I nodded.

We were silent for a minute before I asked, "so, then, what— lack of habitat's causing inbreeding?"

"*No*, it's some kind of *pollution*." My heart hurt from that news. "That's what they said."

"Then, what—the egg shells are too thin?"

"Maybe. **Don't know.** Didn't get **IN to** THAT. They're *busy* out there. I put a hundred bucks in their jar," he continued. "They were grateful, but *I'm almost sorry I did that.*"

"What? Why?"

"Cause after that's when I saw wild, fuckin' squirrels runnin' everywhere—*they're* **savin'** 'em!"

"So?"

"**So**, I **shoot** those damn things all the time. D.C.'s overrun with 'em, pissin' an' crappin', ruinin' houses. Call 'em '*tree rats*,'" he said with disgust. Restoring houses is Erik's business, so, of course, he's seen this. "Won't eat those D.C. Grays. The ones in West Virginia are different, though, got a healthier diet. The limit's six an' they're *delicious*. They're **big** out *there*. We *boil* 'em first, 'cause they're *tough*, ya know? Then, we fry 'em. **Man**, they're *tasty—and tender*. And, they're *beautiful*, too. People mount 'em. They got these *great-big, bushy* tails...." I nodded, without surprise, at this weird news.

"*Oh*," he said with new energy, as he switched tracks." I stopped by the tree and got your blanket. Don't 'spose ya want **that** back," he added with a laugh that I ignored.

"The parents still there?"

"*Oh*, yeah, **they're** there. Think they were sleepin' when *I* showed up. But, they made a couple passes at me. Think they're still lookin' for him."

"Ohhhh, I feel terrible."

"**Why**?"

"They've probably been doing *everything* for him, chewing his food. There have to be reminders—smells, feathers...."

"*Least* he's **alive**. Least they're not looking at him *dead*, in *rotting pieces*. They gotta be *relieved*—The *Fight's* **Over**." There was truth in what he said.

In bed, late that night, I woke to hear a long, hooting sigh and then a reply. I'd never known owls to be so close to my house before. And, I wondered—is it *them*? Are they *still searching*?

2
Firmly Resolved

With Sterling in tow, the White Devil stopped by my porch the next morning to tell me our owl was dead, that they'd *"put him down."*

"Why?" I whispered, as up surged the sickening rush of fear I'd buried about his fate.

"If they can't release 'em better'n they found 'em, can't use 'em for a *'educational animal,'* they put 'em down," Erik told me firmly. My eyes stung, as we three stood, looking at each other.

"But,' I said, "he'd have made a **great** educational animal."

"Go figure," Erik emphasized, as he shook his head. "They *save* the *fuckin'* squirrels and *kill* the *cool* owl."

"No hope for him," Sterling mumbled at Erik's side.

"I thought we *saved* him," I whispered as I saw tears also floating in Sterling's kind eyes. He was **so sad.** "We should have left him, *free,* in his home," I said with regret. "He'd have been happier in the wood —"

*"For **what**,"* the Devil erupted, *"half an hour before he was ripped limb from limb!?"*

"Then," I blurted, *"**I** should have **kept** him."*

"In a **cage**," Erik spat. *"Force fed* and *manhandled* every day of his life!"

"Doomed to a sad life," I whispered over my weak lower lip. "It's *too* sad."

"Yeah," Erik agreed absently before adding with energy, "but only if we look at it that way. Ya know, those kids, even that *stupid* one, are gonna remember that twisted, young owl for the **rest a their lives**."

He was right. And it wasn't just the kids. *I'd* never forget him *either*—sad, silent, soulful, dignified, big-eyed, helpless, and hopeless.

"Ya can't fix *stupid,* but **ignorant** ya can *fix*," Erik continued as his eyes lit up. "That's the **thing**. Somethin' fouls your nest, ya clean it up." The White Devil got more animated as he spoke—shifting on his feet, throwing his hands in the air, tossing his head, nearly snorting with excitement. "And, *those kids*—they're gonna be here *longer'n we* are. We'll *tell* 'em, ya know, 'don't, **don't** dump stuff in the water. Keep crap outta the air. *Remember what it did to the owl and* *don't use that **evil** shit!" If—"*

"Erik," I interrupted, "if we tell those kids what's really happened to that baby owl, we'll make *most* of them *cry*—it could *traumatize* some of them."

"*They* can *take* it," Erik insisted through a frown.

"I'll *tell* the *parents*," I said, "let *them*—"

"The parents *won't do **shit**,*" Erik spit, "'cause *they didn't* **see** it. You're *lyin'* ta yourself. **Stop lyin' ta yourself!**" Then, he pronounced his next words very slowly, making it clear this was the only way he felt his point might seep into my thick skull. "*Ya tell the kids like it* **IS.**"

Erik didn't understand. He had a son graduating high school who'd seen it **all**. Sterling's little boy, however, was only eight.

"Look," I appealed to Sterling, "even if we're the only ones who're more careful because of this, then the little guy wasn't born deformed to live a sad life for nothing."

"If we're **stoppin'** his *tortured life* from **bein'** fer *nothin',*" Erik insisted, "**this** is how we **do** *that!* "

"By making kids cry!" I snapped at him.

"Ya! By makin' kids cry!" he confirmed with force.

"Not the *little* ones," I insisted, knowing full well the older kids would eventually tell the younger ones.

"**The owl's dead,**" Erik yelled over my thoughts. "We *all* killed it. **You** *killed the owl.* Life's tough. *Learn.*"

"Ya *don't* tell them like *that!*" Sterling scolded. "Ya don't tell 'em to **make** 'em cry."

"Not to *make* 'em cry, *no,*" Erik agreed with nearly reasonable volume. "Ya *tell* 'em ta make 'em *better.* If it makes 'em cry, *it makes 'em cry.*"

Locked in frowns, Erik and I cocked our heads at each other, as if facing off in a mirror. "**You** *killed the owl,*" announced by Erik to some crying kid played on in my head.

"I hate to say it," Sterling confessed softly into the stiff air between us, "but I agree with the Devil. *Lyin' makes it worse,*" added the Devil's new advocate.

"*We're doing 'em a* **favor,**" reinforced the Devil. "*It* **helps** 'em," he yelled. "*Hell,* we're doin' nothin' **but** helpin' *tortured lives*—if ya count the worn-out parents **and** the predators they were *rippin'* up! **And**," he emphasized, "**none a them's happy with us either**."

Some good points there, but I shook my head slowly and asked, "Erik, you remember the little girl who wanted to give the owl some tea?" He took a deep breath, paused.

"*Sure*," Erik breathed out through a forced whisper. "*Ya just tell her*," he said seriously, '*they straightened that neck thing right out and the owl's livin' a happy life in some pretty tree somewhere.*'"

That tempting fiction dangled between us, until a quick laugh escaped the Devil like a burp. With a knowing smile, he grew louder. "The three of us'll just use *friendlier* **dish** detergent. It's all *fine and flowers everywhere.*" One corner of his mouth curled as he bit off his message for me—"lyin's what **feels** good, so ya **do** it, **right?**"

I wanted to kick him.

"He **may** get **better**," Sterling reminded me soothingly, "but he'll **never** get *well*." Un-insulted, the Devil stood his ground. He smiled. He was proud of himself.

"We can just tell them that the owl died because it wasn't well," I decided out loud.

"**Everyone** *dies because they're not* **well!**" Erik barked. Another good point, but I didn't let it stop me.

"What was some terrible thing that happened in your childhood, Erik?" I asked. "Something you can't forget, that shaped you? Are you **really willing** to create a memory like that for some kid's lifetime?"

"If that's the lesson that's gotta be learned," Erik answered firmly, "*guess so*. Nature, nurture, somehow, every *thing* and every one's **all** fucked up, it's **all** twisted. Can't ignore it. Gotta know it, gotta learn ta live with it."

"No trouble telling hard truths to the innocent then, *huh*, Erik?" I asked because that was all I had left.

"*None*," he replied with strength. "Even if it hurts, if you're tryin' ta **help** 'em, kids **know** it."

Sterling seemed encouraged by our staring silence. He added with warning, "*but, now*, it's like sweepin' *dried-out leaves* off a *rug*. Gettin' it *done* requires a *light touch*, a bit of *finesse*." He smiled at us, seemed to hope we were pickin' up what he was layin' down. But, echoing in my head was Erik yelling, "**you** *killed the owl!*"

3
Free Your Mind

Don't you see?" Sterling offered to me, softly as a prayer, as we still stood there, on the porch. "It *seems* something people did *wrong* caused the way the owl *formed* to be twisted. Some-how, he lived long enough to make his *way* to the ground, where people *found* him, *tried* to *help* him. If somethin' *good* can come from his *doom*, besides just a *meal or a painless death*, then **there's** the hope. The *hope* **is** in the truth—ya don't tackle a demon by **hidin'** from it."

I remembered the last line of an American-Indian saying that went something like—"tell me, and I may not hear you; show me, and I may not remember; but, *involve* me, and I **will** understand." I connected the dots for myself—owls eat the confused voles, who ate the poisoned grubs, who ate the granulated grub killer I'd sprinkled on the lawn last spring to keep the voles out of my yard. I understood that I, too, killed the owl. And, I understood that involving the kids in the truth of the matter *allowed* them to understand. I was ashamed of myself for trying to cover it up. I felt terrible. My eyes teared up all over again.

"When life's *sad*," Sterling offered kindly, "it's *okay* to cry. In AA, they say, 'if you're *tired*, sleep. If you're *lonely*, call a friend. If you're *hungry*, eat. If you're *thirsty*, drink something *non-alcoholic*.' In other words," he concluded, sounding *so much* like his late father the Reverend, "when the truth is *standin'* there, *starin'* ya *right* in the face—at least *admit it, let it* be true." I nodded, hung my head, con-templated my shoes. Softly, some kind of belch escaped me.

"Excuse me," I whispered. I didn't feel good but I *did* feel better. "Erik's right," I admitted to the floor. The White Devil shifted in his work boots, in the manner of a restrained bull. I looked up to see him smiling triumphantly, nearly bursting from restrained mirth. "*Ya tell 'em like it IS!*" he boasted. I frowned. In my head, I heard Sterling's words from the woods—"Let's *kill* the Viking." The thought, once again, had its appeal.

With the conviction of a southern, street preacher, the White Devil belted-out—"**Free your mind**, and your **OWN** ass'll fol-low!" He laughed maniacally, *almost* evilly. *But, this* time, I heard a cast of *camaraderie*, in his laugh. And, hadn't we *always* known—he wasn't *really* **sooo bad?**

END

Made in the USA
Middletown, DE
02 February 2023